MANAGING YOUR TEAM LIKE A FAMILY

Leadership Lessons From Home

NAVEEN SOOD

BlueRose ONE .com
Stories Matter
NewDelhi • London

BLUEROSE PUBLISHERS
India | U.K.

For permissions requests or inquiries regarding this publication,
please contact:

BLUEROSE PUBLISHERS
www.BlueRoseONE.com
info@bluerosepublishers.com
+91 8882 898 898
+4407342408967

ISBN: 978-93-7018-365-0

Cover Design: Shubham Verma
Typesetting: Sagar

First Edition: March 2025

Managing Your Team Like A Family :

"Leadership Lessons From Home"

By Naveen Sood

About the Author – Naveen Sood

Naveen Sood is a seasoned business leader with over 25 years of experience across various roles—from an engineer to eventually leading sales as a Country Manager. His journey through multiple leadership positions has given him deep insights into team dynamics, workplace challenges, and the importance of fostering a strong organisational culture.

With a rich background in sales, management, and leadership, Naveen believes that the best managers lead their teams the way families function—through trust, empathy, discipline, and support. His hands-on experience in guiding teams has shaped his unique leadership philosophy, which blends professional excellence with personal warmth.

Through this book, Managing Your Team Like a Family: Leadership Lessons from Home, he shares practical strategies for creating a work environment that feels less like a rigid corporate structure and more like a thriving, collaborative family.

Contents

Chapter 1:

Introduction – Managing Teams Like a Family

1.1 Why Compare Family and Corporate Life?

Managing a team is much like managing a family. Both require patience, emotional intelligence, conflict resolution, and the ability to balance different personalities and expectations. Just as a family prosper on communication, trust and mutual support, a workplace flourishes when these elements are in place.

1.2 The Core Idea

In both families and teams:

- Leaders (parents or managers) provide guidance and direction.
- Members (children or employees) require mentorship, training, and motivation.

- External influences (relatives or senior management) offer advice, sometimes supportive, sometimes critical.
- Conflicts arise and need resolution without damaging relationships.

1.3 What This Handbook Will Cover

Each chapter will break down different aspects of leadership by drawing parallels between family roles and corporate structures. By the end of this book, you will have practical strategies to:

- Lead with empathy and clarity.
- Balance expectations from different stakeholders.
- Foster a culture of growth and collaboration.
- Handle conflicts constructively.

1.4 Key Takeaway

"A great leader, like a great family head, nurtures, guides, and adapts—creating an environment where everyone can thrive."

Chapter 2:

The Role of a Manager – Like a Spouse in a Marriage

2.1 The Manager's Role in a Team

A manager is the backbone of any team, just like a spouse is the central figure in a marriage. They are responsible for maintaining balance, resolving conflicts, and ensuring smooth day-to-day operations. Just as a spouse keeps the household running by managing finances, parenting, and emotional well-being, a manager keeps the team productive by setting goals, supporting employees, and fostering a positive work culture.

2.2 Balancing Authority and Empathy

In a marriage, there's a constant balance between making decisions and respecting the partner's opinions. A good spouse doesn't dominate; they **listen, communicate, and collaborate**. Similarly, a great manager leads with authority but also values employee input, creating an environment of mutual respect.

Key Lessons for Managers:

- Don't just give orders—build consensus.
- Be decisive but flexible when needed.
- Treat employees with respect, just as you would a life partner.

2.3 Trust and Communication: The Core of Leadership

A healthy marriage thrives on trust and open communication. If a spouse hides things or makes unilateral decisions, the relationship weakens. The same is true for managers. **Transparency builds trust.** Employees should feel comfortable sharing their challenges without fear.

Practical Tips for Managers:

- Have regular one-on-one check-ins with employees, like daily conversations in a marriage.
- Be open about company goals and expectations.
- Encourage feedback and act on it.

2.4 Handling Conflicts Like a Spouse

Arguments happen in every marriage, but what matters is how they are resolved. A smart spouse listens, understands emotions, and finds middle ground. A manager must do the same—mediate conflicts, ensure fairness, and prevent negative energy from disrupting productivity.

Steps for Conflict Resolution in Teams:

- **Listen to both sides** – Just as a spouse must hear both perspectives before judging.
- **Find the root cause** – Emotions can cloud judgment; focus on facts.
- **Resolve privately, not publicly** – Conflicts should be addressed in private meetings, like personal disagreements in a marriage.

2.5 Supporting Growth and Stability

A good spouse encourages their partner's personal growth while maintaining stability in the household. Similarly, a great manager **develops employees 'skills** while ensuring the team remains aligned with company goals.

How Managers Can Support Growth:

- Provide learning opportunities, like a spouse motivating their partner to improve.
- Recognise achievements to boost morale.
- Encourage autonomy but provide guidance when needed.

2.6 Final Takeaway

"A great manager, like a great spouse, nurtures relationships, fosters trust, and balances structure with empathy. The key to successful leadership lies in understanding, communication, and continuous support."

Chapter 3:

Understanding Team Members – Like Raising Kids

3.1 The Manager as a Guide and Mentor

Just like parents are responsible for their children's growth and development, managers play a crucial role in shaping their employees' careers. Both require **patience, understanding, and the ability to balance discipline with encouragement**. Employees, like children, come with different personalities, strengths, and weaknesses. A good leader recognises these differences and tailors their approach accordingly.

3.2 The Different 'Ages' of Employees

Just as parents handle toddlers, teenagers, and young adults differently, managers must adapt their leadership style to different types of employees.

Employee Type	Family Equivalent	Manager's Role
New Joiners (Freshers)	Toddlers	Provide close guidance, set expectations, and nurture their confidence.
Mid-Level Employees	Teenagers	Give them more independence but correct mistakes constructively.
Senior Team Members	Young Adults	Allow autonomy but offer occasional support when needed.

Lesson: Just as parents gradually give children more freedom as they grow, managers should **delegate responsibility** based on an employee's experience and maturity.

3.3 Training and Development – Like Teaching Kids Life Skills

Children need education, life lessons, and soft skills to succeed. Similarly, employees require continuous **training, mentorship, and skill-building opportunities** to advance in their careers.

Ways to Train Employees Effectively:

- **On-the-job training** – Like teaching kids through real-life experiences.
- **Regular feedback and corrections** – Like parents teaching kids manners and discipline.
- **Encouraging self-learning** – Like children learning from their surroundings and role models.

Lesson: A good parent/manager doesn't just give orders; they teach, guide, and empower their children/team to make the right decisions independently.

3.4 Handling Mistakes – Discipline vs. Encouragement

Children make mistakes, and so do employees. The approach to handling mistakes defines the relationship between a manager and their team.

Just like a parent shouldn't scold a child for every small error, a good manager **corrects employees without demotivating them**.

How to Handle Mistakes Constructively:

- **Understand the intent** – Was it a careless mistake or a learning opportunity?
- **Explain the impact** – Help the employee see why the mistake matters.
- **Encourage corrective action** – Show them how to fix it rather than just pointing out the problem.

Lesson: Over-disciplining can create fear; over-pampering can lead to complacency. A balanced approach builds confident, responsible employees.

3.5 Employee Motivation – Like Encouraging Kids to Succeed

Children thrive on **recognition and encouragement**, whether it's a simple "Well done!" or a reward for good behaviour. Employees are no different. Regular **recognition, appreciation, and motivation** keep them engaged and productive.

Ways to Motivate Employees (Inspired by Parenting Techniques):

- **Praise achievements publicly** – Like celebrating a child's good grades.
- **Give incentives** – Like rewarding kids for good behaviour.
- **Provide growth opportunities** – Like letting kids take on responsibilities at home.

Lesson: A motivated team, like an encouraged child, will put in extra effort and show loyalty when they feel valued.

3.6 Final Takeaway

"Just as great parents guide, train, and inspire their children to grow into responsible adults, ***great managers mentor, support, and develop employees into strong professionals****. The key lies in patience, motivation, and adaptability."*

Chapter 4:

Handling Senior Management – Like Managing In-Laws

4.1 The Role of Senior Management in a Team

Senior management, like in-laws in a family, plays an influential role in shaping decisions, offering advice, and sometimes imposing expectations. They come with experience and authority, but their involvement can sometimes feel overwhelming. Just as a spouse must balance their relationship with their in-laws, a manager must maintain a **respectful yet independent** relationship with senior leadership.

Key Parallels Between Senior Management & In-Laws:

- They have **experience and wisdom** but may not fully understand day-to-day challenges.

- They **set expectations** that managers must align with.
- Their **approval and support** can impact career growth.
- They may sometimes interfere more than necessary, **requiring careful handling.**

4.2 Understanding Their Perspective

Before feeling frustrated with senior management's demands, it's important to understand their **intentions**—just like in-laws, they usually mean well.

Senior Leaders Focus On:

- **Big Picture Thinking** – Like in-laws looking at long-term family well-being.
- **Performance and Results** – Expecting outcomes, not excuses.
- **Company Vision and Stability** – Ensuring traditions and core values are followed.

Lesson: Understanding their perspective helps managers align expectations rather than seeing them as adversaries.

4.3 Managing Expectations – Like Handling In-Laws 'Advice

In-laws may offer advice based on their experiences, sometimes outdated or impractical.

Similarly, senior management might propose strategies that don't fit current realities. The key is to **balance respect and practicality.**

How to Handle Their Advice Diplomatically:

- **Listen actively** – Show respect, even if you don't fully agree.
- **Acknowledge their experience** – Let them know their input is valued.
- **Provide realistic feedback** – Explain why a suggestion may not work and propose alternatives.
- **Keep them informed** – Just like keeping in-laws updated prevents misunderstandings, regularly sharing progress with leadership builds trust.

Example: If senior management pushes for a deadline that seems impossible, instead of saying, "That won't work," try, "We can aim for this target, but we'll need additional resources or a phased approach."

4.4 Gaining Their Trust –

Like Becoming the Favourite Son/Daughter-in-LawWinning over senior management is like earning in-laws 'trust—**through consistent performance, reliability, and respect.**

How to Gain Senior Management's Trust:

- **Deliver on commitments** – Actions speak louder than words.
- **Show initiative** – Offer solutions instead of just raising problems.
- **Maintain transparency** – Keep them informed before they ask.
- **Adapt to their style** – Just like understanding in-laws 'preferences, learn how your leadership prefers communication (detailed reports, short summaries, presentations, etc.).

Lesson: When senior management trusts you, they give you more freedom—just like in-laws stop interfering when they feel their family is in good hands.

4.5 Handling Criticism – Like Dealing with In-Laws 'Complaints

In-laws often compare things to their past experiences and might criticise how things are done differently now. Senior leadership does the same—sometimes comparing past performance, questioning new methods, or demanding perfection.

How to Handle Criticism Professionally:

- Stay calm and don't take it personally.
- Acknowledge their concerns and clarify misunderstandings.
- Show how improvements are being made.
- Be patient—over time, performance will speak for itself.

Example: If senior management criticises a decision, rather than getting defensive, respond with:

"I see your point. Here's why we took this approach, but we can adjust based on your feedback."

4.6 Final Takeaway

"Just as a strong family dynamic requires balancing respect for in-laws with maintaining independence, a successful manager builds a relationship with senior management through trust, transparency, and performance. The goal is to collaborate, not just comply."

Chapter 5:

Handling Owners – Like Managing Parents in a Family

5.1 Owners as Parents – The Ultimate Decision-Makers

In a family, parents **set the rules, provide resources, and guide the household**, just like business owners shape the company's vision, provide funding, and make key decisions. A good manager, much like an elder child or responsible family member, must learn to **balance respect, communication, and independence** while managing expectations.

Owners, like parents, often have **strong emotional investments** in their business. They may have built the company from scratch, just as parents raise children from infancy. This attachment makes them deeply **protective, demanding, and sometimes resistant to change**. A skilled manager understands these emotions and **navigates them with patience and strategic communication**.

5.2 Earning Trust and Respect

Just as children earn their parents 'trust by demonstrating responsibility, managers must **prove their reliability and decision-making skills** to owners. This can be done by:

- Taking ownership of tasks and delivering results consistently
- Keeping the owner informed without unnecessary details
- Showing initiative and problem-solving ability

Owners, like parents, appreciate **loyalty, honesty, and competence**. A manager who aligns with their vision while bringing in fresh ideas earns their confidence.

5.3 Handling High Expectations and Pressure

Owners, like strict parents, may have **unrealistic expectations**, pushing managers to **deliver more with fewer resources**. A good manager must:

- Stay **calm under pressure** and find realistic ways to meet demands
- **Push back respectfully** when needed, providing logical reasons rather than outright refusal
- Manage expectations **without passing stress down to the team**

For example, just as children sometimes negotiate with parents for more independence, managers must convince owners when certain demands are not feasible while offering alternative solutions.

5.4 Bridging the Gap Between Owners and Employees

A manager acts as a **link between the owner and the team**, much like an elder sibling helping younger ones understand parental expectations. Their role includes:

- Translating the owner's vision into actionable steps
- Ensuring the team stays motivated without feeling pressured
- Addressing conflicts and presenting both sides fairly

A good manager, like a responsible family member, must ensure that both **the owners feel respected and the team feels valued**, maintaining balance and harmony in the workplace.

5.5 Knowing When to Seek Approval and When to Act Independently

In families, children learn which decisions require **parental approval** and which they can make on their own. Similarly, managers must:

- **Seek owner's input for critical decisions** that affect strategy, investments, or company reputation
- **Act independently on day-to-day operations**, showing confidence and leadership
- **Take calculated risks** that align with the company's vision, proving their capability

Owners appreciate managers who **take initiative without waiting for constant direction**, just as parents trust grown-up children who handle responsibilities wisely.

Final Takeaway

Managing owners is like managing parents—it requires respect, patience, strategic communication, and trust-building. A great manager, like a mature family member, knows when to listen, when to negotiate, and when to take action, ensuring both the owner's vision and the team's success are aligned.

Chapter 6:

Handling Neighbours as Competitors – Thriving in a Competitive Market

6.1 Understanding Competitors as Neighbours

In a family, neighbours play a dual role—they can be **friends, rivals, or even silent observers.** Some neighbours may offer help and guidance, while others may compete to prove their superiority. Similarly, in business, competitors push companies to **innovate, improve, and stay ahead.**

A good manager understands that competitors, like neighbours:

- **Keep an eye on your progress** – watching your strengths and weaknesses.
- **Compete for resources** – just as neighbours might compare homes, cars, or lifestyle, businesses compete for market share, talent, and customer attention.

- **Can be allies or adversaries** – while some competitors create challenges, others may present opportunities for partnerships or learning.

Instead of fearing competition, a skilled leader **embraces it as motivation** to drive continuous improvement.

6.2 Learning from Competitors Without Imitating

In families, children observe their neighbours—what they do well, what mistakes they make, and how they manage their household. Similarly, businesses must **study their competitors strategically** while maintaining their unique identity.

- **Analyse their strengths and weaknesses** – What do they offer that customers like? Where do they struggle?
- **Differentiate rather than copy** – Instead of blindly following trends, companies should innovate and stand out.
- **Improve based on insights** – Just as families may upgrade their home after seeing a neighbour's renovation, businesses can enhance their offerings by learning from competitors.

The goal is not to outdo competitors at everything but to **play to your own strengths** while understanding their strategies.

6.3 Healthy Competition vs. Unethical Rivalry

Some neighbours engage in **healthy, respectful competition**, while others might resort to jealousy, gossip, or underhanded tactics. The same applies to business competitors—some companies innovate ethically, while others engage in **price wars, misinformation, or aggressive tactics.**

A responsible manager ensures that their company:

- Competes ethically – Winning by delivering better products/services, not by misleading customers.
- Maintains professionalism – Not getting distracted by personal rivalries.
- Responds strategically – Rather than reacting emotionally, using data-driven strategies to counter competitor moves.

Just as wise families ignore negative gossip from neighbours, businesses should focus on internal strengths rather than worrying about every competitor's move.

6.4 Collaborating with Competitors When Necessary

Sometimes, neighbours **join hands for a common goal**—whether it's organising a festival or handling a community issue. Similarly, businesses can find **opportunities to collaborate with competitors** in mutually beneficial ways.

- **Industry alliances** – Competitors can work together to set industry standards or improve market practices.
- **Cooperative Competition** – Partnering on shared resources while still maintaining distinct customer bases.
- **Acquisitions & Partnerships** – If a competitor's strength complements your weakness, collaboration can lead to growth.

Knowing when to compete and when to collaborate is **a mark of a mature business leader.**

6.5 Staying Ahead – Becoming a Market Leader

The best way to handle competitors is **to stay ahead of them.** A good manager ensures their company:

- Continuously innovates – Keeping up with market trends and customer needs.
- Focuses on brand loyalty – Building strong relationships so customers stick with them.
- Develops a strong team – Creating a culture of motivation, learning, and adaptability.

Instead of fearing competition, businesses should use it as motivation to become stronger and more innovative.

Final Takeaway

Competitors, like neighbours, can be rivals, inspirations, or even partners. The key is to stay aware, stay ethical, and stay ahead. Businesses that focus on continuous growth, strategic differentiation, and strong customer relationships will always come out stronger in the long run.

Chapter 7:

Team Collaboration – Like Sibling Relationships

7.1 Why Team Collaboration Feels Like Sibling Bonds

A team, like siblings, grows together, competes, supports each other, and sometimes argues. Just as siblings share responsibilities in a family, team members contribute to the success of a project. While conflicts are inevitable, strong collaboration leads to a productive and harmonious workplace.

Parallels Between Siblings and Team Members:

- **Healthy competition** – Siblings compete for attention; employees compete for promotions.
- **Shared responsibilities** – Household chores vs. team tasks.

- **Conflicts and misunderstandings** – Disagreements arise but must be managed constructively.
- **Support during challenges** – Just like siblings back each other up, strong teams step in when needed.

7.2 Encouraging Healthy Competition

Competition among siblings can be both motivating and frustrating. The key is to **encourage growth without creating rivalry**. The same applies in a team—employees should strive for excellence without undermining each other.

How Managers Can Foster Positive Competition:

- **Recognise individual strengths** – Ensure everyone feels valued.
- **Encourage peer learning** – Promote knowledge-sharing rather than secretive competition.
- **Reward collaboration, not just individual success** – Balance promotions and bonuses with team-based rewards.

Example: Instead of ranking employees against each other, managers can set **team-based**

goals where collaboration leads to shared success.

7.3 Resolving Team Conflicts – Like Sibling Fights

Siblings often argue over small things, just like colleagues disagree over responsibilities or recognition. The key to resolving conflicts is ensuring **fairness and open communication**.

Steps to Handle Team Conflicts:

- **Identify the root cause** – Is it workload imbalance, recognition issues, or personal differences?
- **Encourage direct conversation** – Like parents telling siblings to talk it out.
- **Mediate when needed** – Step in if conflicts affect performance.
- **Focus on solutions, not blame** – Keep discussions productive.

Lesson: Healthy debates improve ideas, but unresolved conflicts damage team spirit. A good leader, like a parent, must mediate fairly.

7.4 Promoting Teamwork – Like Family Bonding Activities

Families strengthen bonds through shared meals, trips, and traditions. Similarly, **team-building activities** help employees connect beyond work.

Ways to Strengthen Team Collaboration:

- **Encourage informal interactions** – Casual chats build relationships.
- **Organise team outings or virtual meet-ups** – Strengthens personal connections.
- **Celebrate successes together** – Acknowledge collective achievements.

Example: Just like family game nights bring siblings closer, **team-building exercises** improve communication and trust.

7.5 Supporting Each Other – Like Siblings During Tough Times

Siblings may fight, but they stand together in difficult times. A strong team does the same—**supporting struggling colleagues rather than competing against them.**

How to Build a Supportive Team Culture:

- **Encourage knowledge sharing** – Seniors should mentor juniors.
- **Promote collaboration over individual wins** – Success should be shared.
- **Recognise teamwork publicly** – Praise those who help others.

Lesson: A team that supports each other grows together, just like siblings who eventually become lifelong allies.

7.6 Final Takeaway

"Just as siblings grow through competition, support, and shared experiences, a great team thrives on healthy collaboration, fairness, and mutual respect."

Chapter 8:

Motivation and Recognition – Like Encouraging Kids

8.1 Why Motivation Matters

In a family, children perform better when they are encouraged, appreciated, and given responsibilities. Similarly, employees thrive when their efforts are recognised, their hard work is acknowledged, and they feel valued.

A workplace without motivation is like a household where parents never praise their kids—**eventually, enthusiasm fades, and performance suffers**. Managers, like parents, need to create an environment where employees feel inspired to give their best.

8.2 Types of Workplace Motivation

1. Intrinsic Motivation – The Desire to Do Well

This is the internal drive to succeed, similar to how some kids love learning because they enjoy the challenge. Employees with intrinsic motivation:

- Take initiative and go beyond their tasks.
- Feel proud of their work, even without external rewards.
- Thrive in roles that allow creativity and ownership.

Manager's Role: Encourage autonomy, assign meaningful tasks, and provide positive reinforcement.

2. Extrinsic Motivation – Rewards and Recognition

Just as children are motivated by gifts, prizes, or appreciation, employees respond to external recognition. This can include:

- **Financial rewards:** Bonuses, salary hikes, incentives.
- **Public recognition:** Employee of the month, appreciation in meetings.
- **Career growth opportunities:** Promotions, training, leadership roles.

Manager's Role: Balance financial and non-financial incentives to keep motivation high.

8.3 Balancing Praise and Constructive Feedback

Encouragement doesn't mean overlooking mistakes. Just as parents correct their children's behaviour while still motivating them, managers must provide **constructive feedback without demoralising employees**.

The Right Way to Give Feedback:

- **Recognise effort, not just results** – Praise hard work, even if the outcome isn't perfect.
- **Be specific** – Instead of saying *"Good job,"* say *"Your detailed report helped us close the deal."*
- **Balance criticism with encouragement** – Highlight strengths before addressing areas of improvement.
- **Make feedback a two-way conversation** – Employees should feel involved, not attacked.

8.4 The Power of Celebrating Success Together

In families, we celebrate birthdays, achievements, and milestones to make members feel valued. Workplaces should do the same!

Ways to Celebrate Employee Achievements:

🎉 Team lunches or informal gatherings.

🏆 Awards and certificates.

📢 Public appreciation in company meetings.

📈 Promotions and leadership opportunities.

Manager's Role: Build a **culture of appreciation** where employees feel recognised not just for big wins but also for small contributions.

8.5 Final Takeaway

"Just as children perform better when appreciated, employees give their best when they feel valued. A motivated team is a productive team—recognition fuels engagement, loyalty, and long-term success."

Chapter 9:

Dealing with Difficult Employees – Like Handling Stubborn Relatives

9.1 Why Some Employees Are Difficult

Every family has that one stubborn relative who resists advice, ignores responsibilities, or disrupts harmony. Similarly, workplaces have difficult employees—those who underperform, resist feedback, create negativity, or refuse to work as a team.

While it's easy to ignore the problem or react emotionally, a good manager, like a wise family member, **deals with issues calmly and strategically** to maintain a healthy work environment.

9.2 Types of Difficult Employees and How to Manage Them

1. The Resistant Employee " –I've always done it this way!"

These employees refuse to adapt to new methods or changes, just like a grandparent who insists on following old traditions.

How to Handle:

- Explain the "**why**" behind changes.
- Show patience—change takes time.
- Give **small responsibilities** to ease them into new ways.

2. The Negative Influencer " –This place is a mess!"

This person constantly complains, demotivates others, and spreads negativity—similar to a family member who always criticises but never offers solutions.

How to Handle:

- Address the behaviour directly and privately.
- Ask them to propose solutions instead of just complaining.
- Surround them with positive team members.

3. The Under performer " –I just can't do this."

Like a child struggling in school, these employees lack confidence, skills, or motivation.

How to Handle:

- Identify if it's a skill gap or motivation issue.
- Provide training and support.
- Set clear performance expectations and milestones.

4. The Lone Wolf " –I work better alone."

Some employees don't like teamwork, just like some family members avoid gatherings.

How to Handle:

- Find **individual tasks** that suit their strengths.
- Gradually involve them in **team activities.**
- Assign **a mentor or buddy** to ease collaboration.

9.3 When to Take Strict Action – Like Setting Family Discipline

Some behaviours, if left unchecked, can damage the team's morale. Just as parents set rules for children, managers must establish **boundaries and consequences** for unacceptable behaviour.

Situations That Require Firm Action:

- ⚐ Repeated disrespect or conflicts.
- ⚐ Lack of accountability despite coaching.
- ⚐ Toxic behaviour affecting the team.

Manager's Role: Be clear, fair, and firm. If needed, take disciplinary action or part ways.

9.4 Final Takeaway

"Not everyone will align with the team. Like in a family, knowing when to guide, when to tolerate, and when to set boundaries is key to leadership."

Chapter 10:

Conflict Resolution – Like Handling Family Disputes

10.1 Why Conflicts Are Inevitable

Conflicts arise in both families and workplaces because people have different personalities, expectations, and ways of working. Just like in a family, workplace conflicts can stem from misunderstandings, competition, personal differences, or unclear responsibilities. A well-managed conflict can lead to **growth, better relationships, and stronger teamwork**, while unresolved issues can cause long-term resentment.

Parallels Between Family Disputes and Workplace Conflicts

- **Sibling Rivalries → Team Member Competitions** (Who gets promoted first, who gets more recognition)

- **Parent-Child Differences → Manager-Employee Disagreements** (Authority vs. independence)
- **Extended Family Clashes → Interdepartmental Conflicts** (Different teams with different priorities)

The key to handling conflicts—whether in a family or at work—is **fairness, active listening, and solution-driven conversations**.

10.2 Steps to Resolving Workplace Conflicts

1. Listen to Both Sides – Like a Parent Resolving a Sibling Fight

Just like parents listen to both children before deciding who is right, a manager should hear out all parties without bias. **Encouraging open communication helps prevent misunderstandings.**

2. Identify the Root Cause – Emotion vs. Real Issue

In families, an argument about dinner plans may actually be about deeper issues like feeling unheard. Similarly, a workplace conflict about workload may stem from an employee feeling undervalued. **Understanding the real reason behind a conflict is key to solving it.**

3. Encourage Open and Honest Communication

- Set up **private discussions** instead of public confrontations.
- Use **neutral language** to avoid escalating tensions.
- Guide employees to **focus on solutions**, not just blame.

4. Mediate Fairly – Stay Neutral Like a Family Elder

A good leader is like a respected elder in the family—someone who **doesn't take sides but ensures fairness**. Encourage both parties to **find common ground** and **compromise where needed**.

5. Follow Up to Ensure Resolution

In families, apologies don't always mean the issue is resolved—there may still be lingering emotions. In workplaces, after resolving a conflict, **check in after a few days** to ensure things are truly settled.

10.3 Setting Boundaries to Prevent Future Conflicts

Just like family rules prevent unnecessary fights, **clear workplace policies** help avoid misunderstandings.

How Managers Can Prevent Repeated Conflicts:

- Define roles and expectations clearly.
- Encourage respect in communication.
- Create a culture of openness where employees feel safe discussing issues early.

Example: In a family, if two siblings constantly fight over TV time, setting a schedule solves the problem. In the workplace, if employees argue over shared resources, **a clear policy on resource allocation prevents future disputes**.

10.4 When to Take Strict Action – Like Setting Family Discipline

Some conflicts can't be solved with just discussions. Just as **parents step in with discipline when needed**, managers sometimes have to enforce workplace rules.

Situations That Require Strict Action:

- Repeated misconduct or toxic behaviour.

- Harassment or disrespectful language.
- Affecting team morale and productivity.

A balance of fairness and firmness helps maintain harmony.

10.5 Final Takeaway

"Just like family disputes, workplace conflicts should be handled with patience, fairness, and long-term harmony in mind. A great leader is like a good family elder—neutral, fair, and focused on unity."

Chapter 11:

Work-Life Balance – Like Managing Family Expectations

11.1 The Struggle of Balancing Work and Home

Balancing work and personal life is like managing both your professional and family responsibilities. Just as a parent needs to juggle household chores, kids 'education, and social commitments, an employee must handle deadlines, meetings, and personal well-being.

When either side is neglected, problems arise—**work stress affects home life, and personal issues impact work performance**. A good manager, like a responsible family member, must encourage balance to ensure long-term productivity and happiness.

11.2 Parallels Between Work-Life Balance and Family Responsibilities

Family Situation	Work Situation
Parents ensuring children get enough rest, study time, and playtime.	Managers promoting a balance between work hours, learning, and breaks.
Handling family disputes calmly without taking extreme steps.	Managing workplace challenges without unnecessary escalation.
Setting family routines to create stability.	Encouraging structured work schedules for efficiency.
Supporting a spouse's career choices while managing household responsibilities.	Encouraging employees' professional growth while respecting their personal lives.

Just as a family functions best when responsibilities are shared and expectations are realistic, a workplace thrives when employees are given the space to balance their personal and professional lives.

11.3 The Role of Managers in Work-Life Balance

A good manager is like a family head who ensures that no one feels overburdened. They must:

- **Encourage Time Management:** Help employees prioritise tasks so they don't carry work stress home.
- **Promote Flexibility:** Offer remote work or flexible hours where possible.
- **Lead by Example:** Avoid sending late-night emails or expecting employees to be available 24/7.
- **Respect Personal Time:** Just like weekends and holidays are family time, employees should have protected personal time.

Example: A manager who understands an employee's need to leave early for a family commitment builds trust and loyalty, just as a supportive spouse or parent strengthens a family bond.

11.4 Avoiding Burnout – Like Preventing Family Exhaustion

In families, constant stress can lead to emotional breakdowns. Similarly, **overworked employees face burnout, reducing productivity and creativity.**

How to Prevent Workplace Burnout:

- **Recognise signs early** – fatigue, lack of motivation, frustration.
- **Encourage regular breaks** – even short pauses improve focus.
- **Foster an open culture** – employees should feel comfortable discussing stress without fear.
- **Distribute workload fairly** – avoid burdening top performers while others to coast.

Example: Just as a mother delegates chores among children so one isn't overworked, managers should ensure fair work distribution.

11.5 The Importance of Personal Growth Outside Work

A happy employee is one who has a **fulfilling life outside work.** Encourage employees to:

- Pursue hobbies and fitness to refresh their minds.
- Learn new skills beyond work, such as music, cooking, or sports.
- Spend quality time with family to recharge emotionally.

Example: A father who takes time to play with his kids after work feels refreshed. Similarly, an employee who has personal time returns to work more focused and energised.

11.6 Final Takeaway

"Just as a family thrives when responsibilities are shared and time is managed well, employees perform best when they are encouraged to balance their work and personal lives."

Chapter 12 :

Handling Diversity – Caste, Gender, and Inclusion in Teams

12.1 Recognising Workplace Diversity

Just like a family embraces differences in personalities, strengths, and roles, a workplace is diverse in many aspects—caste, gender, culture, and background. A good leader ensures that these differences become strengths rather than sources of division.

12.2 Caste and Cultural Sensitivities in the Workplace

In many organisations, employees come from different social and cultural backgrounds. A strong manager, like a family head, fosters an inclusive environment where merit and teamwork outweigh social biases. Encouraging collaboration and mutual respect among team members builds a healthy work culture.

12.3 Gender Equality – Balancing Roles Like in a Family

- **Women in Leadership** – In families, mothers often play central leadership roles. Similarly, workplaces should empower female employees by providing equal opportunities, leadership roles, and a supportive environment.
- **Breaking Stereotypes** – Just as modern families share responsibilities irrespective of gender, a progressive workplace assigns roles based on skills and competence rather than gender norms.

12.4 Creating an Inclusive Workplace

- **Respect Differences** – Like a family values each member's individuality, a workplace should celebrate diverse perspectives.
- **Provide Equal Growth Opportunities** – Ensure promotions, increments, and responsibilities are given based on performance, not bias.
- **Zero Tolerance for Discrimination** – Foster a culture where any form of discrimination is addressed immediately.

12.5 Final Takeaway

A workplace, like a home, thrives on fairness and inclusivity. A good leader ensures that caste, gender, or social background never become barriers, just as a strong family values each member equally. Managing with fairness and empathy creates a stronger, more united team.

Chapter 13:

Mentorship and Succession Planning – Like Passing Family Values to the Next Generation

13.1 The Role of Mentorship in Organisations

Just as parents and elders in a family guide younger generations, mentorship in a workplace helps employees develop skills, gain confidence, and grow into leadership roles. Effective mentorship ensures that knowledge and values are passed down, creating a culture of continuous learning and stability.

13.2 The Importance of Succession Planning

In families, parents prepare their children to take responsibility as they grow older. Similarly, businesses must plan for leadership transitions to ensure continuity. A strong succession plan identifies future leaders, provides them with training, and ensures the company remains stable even when key leaders step down.

13.3 Key Elements of Effective Mentorship

- **Guidance and Support:** Managers should act as mentors, helping employees navigate challenges and build their careers.
- **Constructive Feedback:** Like parents correct and encourage their children, leaders should provide regular feedback to improve performance.
- **Skill Development:** Employees should be given opportunities to learn new skills, just as children are encouraged to develop talents.
- **Building Confidence:** Encouraging employees to take initiative, solve problems, and make decisions, similar to how parents teach children independence.

13.4 Steps to Create a Strong Succession Plan

- **Identify Potential Leaders:** Recognize employees with leadership qualities and invest in their growth.

- **Provide Training and Exposure:** Give them opportunities to handle critical tasks and learn from senior leaders.
- **Encourage Knowledge Sharing:** Ensure experienced employees pass down expertise, just as elders teach family traditions.
- **Develop a Transition Plan:** When a leadership change is near, provide proper handover and gradual responsibility transfer.

13.5 The Long-Term Benefits of Mentorship and Succession Planning

- **Ensures Business Continuity:** The company remains strong even when leadership changes.
- **Builds Employee Loyalty:** Employees feel valued and see growth opportunities, reducing turnover.
- **Creates a Culture of Learning:** Employees constantly improve, benefiting the company's future.

Final Takeaway

Like a well-prepared family that nurtures and guides its next generation, businesses must invest in mentorship and structured succession planning. A workplace that actively supports growth and transition creates strong, capable leaders and ensures long-term success.

Chapter 14:

The Final Message – Leading with Empathy and Authority

A workplace, much like a family, thrives on a foundation of **trust, respect, and mutual support**. Just as a family leader nurtures relationships, sets boundaries, and guides their children toward independence, a great manager must do the same for their team. **Authority provides structure, while empathy fosters connection**, and both are essential to creating a thriving, high-performing work environment.

A company's long-term success depends not only on achieving short-term results but also on **building a culture where employees feel valued, motivated, and empowered**. Employees who feel trusted, respected, and supported are more likely to be engaged, productive, and committed to the organization's goals.

14.1 Balancing Authority and Empathy in Leadership

Just as parents must discipline their children with fairness and understanding, managers must enforce policies and expectations **without losing the human touch**. A strong leader is not just someone who **commands and controls** but also someone who **guides, supports, and inspires**.

- **Empathy** helps employees feel safe, understood, and motivated to do their best.
- **Authority** ensures that work gets done efficiently, with discipline and accountability.
- **The right balance** creates an environment where people are both **challenged and supported**, much like in a well-functioning family.

A workplace that lacks empathy may feel cold and robotic, while one that lacks authority may become chaotic and unproductive. The key is to **blend the two**, just as a parent knows when to be firm and when to be nurturing.

14.2 How Leaders Can Foster a Family-Like Culture at Work

- **Be Approachable and Open to Communication** – Just as family members turn to each other for advice and support, employees should feel comfortable seeking guidance from their leaders.
- **Lead by Example** – Like a parent who models good behaviour for their children, a leader must demonstrate integrity, discipline, and dedication.
- **Create a Safe and Inclusive Environment** – Just as a home should be a safe space, a workplace should be a place where employees feel secure, respected, and valued.
- **Encourage Growth and Independence** – Great leaders, like great parents, **prepare people for bigger responsibilities** by offering training, mentorship, and opportunities to develop new skills.
- **Recognise Effort and Celebrate Success** – Just as a child thrives on encouragement, employees need to feel appreciated for their contributions.

14.3 Building a Lasting and Engaged Workforce

A successful workplace doesn't just focus on immediate tasks—it builds a **sustainable culture** where people are motivated to stay and grow. Companies with high employee engagement **experience better performance, lower turnover, and stronger team morale**.

When leaders lead with **empathy and authority**, they create more than just great employees—they build **a community of committed professionals** who take ownership of their work and contribute positively to the organisation.

Final Thought:

"A company's success is not just measured by profits, but by the strength of its people. Just as a loving family grows together through trust and guidance, a thriving organisation flourishes when leaders balance structure with support, and authority with empathy."